Kingdom Character Citizenship Training

**TOUCHING LIVES WITH THE REALITY
OF KINGDOM DOMINION**

VOLUME 1

TERANCE AND VICTORIA BLOUNT

Kingdom Character Citizenship Training

Copyright © 2021 by TERANCE AND VICTORIA BLOUNT

All rights reserved. No part of this book may be reproduced or transmitted in any form or by any means without written permission from the author.

ISBN: 978-0-578-91020-8

Kingdom Character Citizenship Training

Holiness/Righteousness of God's Kingdom Living

Luke 1:75 KJV - "In holiness and righteousness before him, all the days of our life."

Romans 11:29 - "For the gifts and calling of God are without repentance."

Table of Contents

FORWARD 1

INTRODUCTION 3

REDISCOVERING SIX CHARACTERISTIC ATTRIBUTES 10

    Inside the Box 14

    Spiritual Courage 14

    MORAL COURAGE 17

    The Big Mirror: 22

    Self-Evaluation 22

    Putting Yourself in the Mirror 37

    Endurance. 39

WE ARE WINNERS! 43

    Processing Endurance 45

    Exercising Endurance Through Discipline 47

    Sharpening Your Focus in the Mirror 51

    Emptiness of the Inner Man (Soul) 52

    Fulfillment of the Inner Man (Soul). 55

About The Blounts 58

Biblical References 59

FORWARD

Kingdom Character Citizenship Training

I have desired a teaching of this type for many years. It is so well organized and scripturally accurate that you will see Jesus, not church or religion. The tools that we need are presented in such a way that it penetrates beyond the intellectual, religious surface stuff and develops heart living. It is evident that many years of labor and prayer have been spent before the Lord for this consistent approach.

The Blounts

I thank the Lord for bringing these vessels into our lives. They have truly been a gift to my wife, our church, and myself. So, encouraging resourceful and most of all LOVING. I cannot wait for this training to take place at our churches, they are so smooth!

Apostle Fred Harris
New Risen Christ Ministries International
Detroit, MI 48033

Apostle Terance and Victoria Blount, have represented Christ to ministries and congregations internationally. Their lives exemplify Godly character, poise, and the Kingdom Citizenship mandate.

As you read the manual, the practical application will draw you into the mind of Christ and the character of Father/God. I believe you will experience deep calls to deep in this rich anointed content.
Your inner man will be strengthened with power through His Spirit.

We are honored to make this small contribution to this book. I believe this book is going to be a special blessing to those who desire to have a Kingdom Citizenship Character.

Pastors Kevin and Angel Kelley

Royal Priesthood Worship Courts

Dover, Delaware

INTRODUCTION

Welcome to Small Group Character Development Training. The purpose of the training is to re-establish intimacy with God. ***Proverbs 11:1 KJV, "a false balance is an abomination to the Lord, but a just weight is his delight."***

1 Corinthians 3:1-3 KJV, "And I brethren, could not speak unto you as unto spiritual, but as unto carnal, even as unto babes in Christ. 2) I have fed you with milk, and not with meat: for hitherto ye were not able to bear it, neither yet now are ye able. 3) For ye are yet carnal: for whereas there is among you envying, and strife, and divisions, are ye not carnal, and walk as men?"

Unbalance has caused many divisions in the House of worship, and man-made doctrines have done the same in the Body of Christ. It is a sickness because believers in Christ exercise their gifts and talents in the fullness of their desires, rather than living a holy and righteous life of Christ Jesus. For instance, let us talk about a *Carnal* Christian; we hear the term all the time but do not mention it much in our teachings. The Bible calls a believer that acts like a non-believer a carnal Christian. The word carnal means to be **fleshly and temporal or earthly**. Carnal behaviors are motivated by the lust of the eyes, lust of the flesh, and pride of life. The topic of carnal relationships is a subject that man, woman, boy or girl want to know more about, but both children and parents may be embarrassed to talk about it with each other. It refers to the natural man as opposed to the spiritual man. When we use the word carnal, we mean *"The flesh,"* which is influenced by the world's system's ways rather than God's kingdom's influence. It also refers to cravings after the things of the **flesh**, **attraction**, and **satisfaction.** *According to Matthew 6:33 AMP, "But first and most importantly seek (aim at, strive after) His kingdom and His righteousness [His way of doing and being right—the attitude and character of God], and all these things will be given to you also."* Every Born-again Believer must first seek God's Kingdom to understand their citizenship position by His Grace. Our carnal thoughts are influenced by the kingdom of darkness that emerges through our senses. It affects how our **minds, will,** and

emotions respond in the visible realm rather than the spiritual. When they attempt to be more transparent towards a mature believer, the response will come from correction of one's thought process and thinking about a particular subject matter or just in a normal conversation.

Today, we see all over the world, especially in the United States of America, The Lord is moving on the earth, and He is moving through His remnant to preach the Good News, the Gospel of the Kingdom, restoring His Image and likeness in the Church. While being activated using our gifts, our character is critical for our survival in kingdom maturity. Our Heavenly Father desires a relationship with us and cares deeply about our image and likeness of Him. We must grow from religion (*man-made*) to a relationship (*intimacy*) with Him.

Ephesians 5:1,2 NIV, *"Be imitators of God, therefore, as dearly loved children, and live a life of love, just as Christ Jesus loved us and gave himself up for us as a fragrant offering and sacrifice to The Lord.*" Having a balanced lifestyle will cause our walk with The Lord to become more fruitful in our place of worship, in the marketplaces, in our community, and in other surrounding areas where we can be effective. As Kingdom Ambassadors, He desires complete obedience to His **'Will.'**

Self-Reflection:

It is like looking into a mirror and describing what you see; in other words, assessing yourself when pressure is applied to you.

If there must be a balance between gift and character, then let us define character?

I. Define Character: **(the inner core of the human being; conscience)**

1. It is the seat of one's moral being **(right and wrong in human behavior moral problems a moral judgment)**
2. It is the inner soul of man **(male/female – spiritual or personal aspect of a person)**
    a. It will reflect either the traits of the sinful nature **(being influenced by the world)**
    b. It is the traits of the divine nature **(being influenced by the Gospel of the Kingdom, the Word of God)**
3. It is the combination of qualities distinguishing any person or class of persons. **(individuality)**

4. It is displayed in the action of an individual under pressure **(stress and pressure)**. <u>Stress</u> – is when the demands of our environment outweigh our (perceived) ability to respond. Our daily lives' challenges make us feel threatened; we don't have the time, patience, energy, or income to meet our desires.

5. <u>Pressure</u> – is a situation that can have significant and negative results if you don't perform well under pressure. It feels like a life-or-death situation, reputation, relationship, business, ministry success, or feeling safe around family or friends.

6. Lastly, it is the combined total of all the Negative and Positive qualities in a person's life, exemplified by one's
   a. Thoughts – *Psalms 139:2 NIV* (Emphasis Here)
   b. Values – *Psalms 109:21 - 31 NIV* (Emphasis Here)
   c. Motivations – *Hebrew 12:9 - 11 NIV* (Emphasis Here)
   d. Attitudes – *Ephesians 4:22, 23 NIV* (Emphasis Here)
   e. Feelings – *Romans 12:1 - 8 KJV* (Emphasis Here)
   f. Actions – *James 2:17 NIV* (Emphasis Here)

II. **Attitude of Behavior**: **(religion)**
   1. *It is what a person will ideally be in the near future.*
      a. It is what a person is at this present time.
      b. When the pressure of life comes to a person's life, the true person surfaces
      c. A person may act and think one way under the blessings of the Lord, but a different type of attitude when the trials and heat of their circumstances catch them by surprise.

   2. *Learned Behavior is how a person acts from another person actions:*
      a. It includes a person's inner thoughts, motives, and attitudes
      b. Thoughts, though hidden, indicate the true character of a person
      c. Motives, too, are true expressions of the inner soul of man **(male/female)**
      d. To change the behavior of a person, one must go deeper than action

3. ***The nature of God does not appear without pressure:***
    a. The **pressures** of life test what the Lord has accomplished in a person's character (2Corinthians 1:8)
    b. When the heat is upon a person's character, his or her true nature surfaces *(Jeremiah 17:8)*
    c. The common irritations of everyday living expose the weaknesses in every person's life *(Romans 8:26)*
    d. It forms under pressure and circumstances *(2 Corinthians 11:28)*
    e. The qualities that are truly part of a person's character are consistent, whether the heat is on or off their life. *(1 Corinthians 10:13)*

4. ***Learned Behavior is that which other people see on the external. (Matthew 23:25)***
    a. It is what other people do not see.
    b. People may see only the side of a person they want to display, but God sees the real you.
    c. An individual cannot hide his or her weaknesses from The Lord.
    d. Humanity may look at the external, but The Lord looks at the heart.
    e. The Lord commands good works from each of us, and it must proceed out of a kingdom character.
    f. A person can do many outward religious works and still be unrighteous.
    g. Works are not always a sign of holiness and righteousness.

5. ***Character is not limited to having wisdom to comment on the behavior of others. (Romans 12:1, 2)***
    a. Intellectually knowing how to act, think and feel consistently with kingdom principles may be a far cry from living in harmony with those principles.
    b. A person with kingdom character doesn't just verbally tell other people what to do, but they live as an example worthy of following.

6. **Character is not limited to relationships between Saints.** *(1 Corinthians 15:30)*
   a. To believe that it does not matter how a saint acts toward a non-believer is a deception.
   b. Character shows forth kingdom principles in every situation and toward all people.
   (Example: A Born-again employee must give the same respect to another employee no matter what attitude or behavior they display)

7. *Character is not limited to a person's relationship with his spiritual family. It also shows in how he or she treats his or her natural family. (Proverbs 27:11)*
   a. A Saint must demonstrate their faith and love the same way they do with their own immediate family.
   b. A person's kingdom character can be discerned by how they respect and honor their father and mother.
   c. A Saint with an unbelieving natural family can win his or her family to Christ by having a mature and loving character toward them.

NOTE: *All disciples must remember when a challenge comes in your pathway:*

What If?
That's the Question?

If you create an **attitude**,
you inherit a **learned behavior**.

If you create a **learned behavior,**
you inherit a **character**.

If you create a **character**,
you inherit your **destiny**."

What is learned behavior?

_____

_____

Give two examples of learned behavior:

_____

_____

III.   *Character is a MUST in our Holy Lifestyle. (1 Thessalonians 4:7)*

You will find that it warns of an onslaught of wickedness and perversity in the Earth's last days when researching the scriptures. This great onslaught only increases our need for kingdom character. The standards of this world system are becoming more wicked as the days pass by.

What does this statement mean; *"The Lord will raise up a people with the righteousness of Christ Jesus?"*

_____

How?

_____

A Kingdom lifestyle will testify to the power of the Holy Spirit in your life. While this world's character and behavior become more corrupt and evasive, the Lord is causing His Ministers and Ministries' character and conduct to mature. We need to be developed in the likeness of Jesus to resist being conformed into this world's systems.

Romans 12:2 AMP, "And do not be conformed to this world **[any longer with its superficial values and customs]**, but be transformed and progressively changed **[as you mature spiritually]** by the renewing of your mind **[focusing on godly values and ethical attitudes]**, so that you may prove **[for ourselves]** what the will of God is, that which is good and acceptable and perfect **[in His plan and purpose for you]**."

If we are to achieve and retain the image of our Lord, then we must allow ourselves room for preparation and testing for us to lead the way. We must develop strong, kingdom character to stand against the enemy's attacks (Kingdom of Satan).

Ephesians 6:12-17 AMP, "For our struggle is not against flesh and blood **[contending only with physical opponents]**, but against the rulers, against the powers, against the world forces of this **[present]** darkness, against the spiritual forces of wickedness in the heavenly **(supernatural)** places. (**13**) Therefore, put on the complete armor of God, so that you will be able to **[successfully]** resist and stand your ground in the evil day **[of danger]**, and having done everything **[that the crisis demands]**, to stand firm **[in your place, fully prepared, immovable, victorious]**. (**14**) So stand firm and hold your ground, having tightened the wide band of truth **[personal integrity, moral courage]** around your waist and having put on the breastplate of righteousness **[an upright heart]**, (**15**) and having strapped on your feet the gospel of peace in preparation **[to face the enemy with firm-footed stability and the readiness produced by the good news.]** (**16**) Above all, lift up the **[protective]** shield of faith with which you can extinguish all the flaming arrows of the evil one. (**17**) And take the helmet of salvation, and the sword of the Spirit, which is the Word of God."

Rediscovering Six Characteristic Attributes

1. Courage.

Be Strong and of Good Courage

Joshua 1:1 – 15 ERV – **1)** Moses was the Lord's servant, and Joshua, son of Nun, was Moses' helper. After Moses died, the Lord spoke to Joshua and said, **2)** "My servant Moses is dead. Now you and all these people must go across the Jordan River. You must go into the land I am giving to the Israelites. **3)** I promised Moses that I would give you this land, so I will give you all the land wherever you go. **4)** All the land from the desert to Lebanon all the way to the great river **(that is, the Euphrates River)** and all the land of the Hittites will be yours. And all the land from here to the Mediterranean Sea in the west **(that is, the place where the sun sets)** will be within your borders. **5)** Just as I was with Moses, I will be with you. No one will be able to stop you all your life. I will not abandon you. I will never leave you. **6)** "Joshua, you must be strong and brave! You must lead these people so that they can take their land. I promised their fathers that I would give them this land. **7)** But you must be strong and brave about obeying the commands my servant Moses gave you. If you follow his teachings exactly, you will be successful in everything you do. **8)** Always remember what is written in that book of the law. Speak about that book and study it day and night. Then you can be sure to obey what is written there. If you do this, you will be wise and successful in everything you do. **9)** Remember, I commanded you to be strong and brave. Don't be afraid because the Lord your God will be with you wherever you go." **10)** So Joshua gave orders to the leaders of the people: **11)** "Go through the camp and tell the people, 'Get some food ready. Three days from now we will go across the Jordan River and take the land that the Lord our God is giving us." **12)** Then Joshua said to the tribes of Reuben, Gad, and half the tribe of Manasseh, **13)** "Remember what the Lord servant Moses has told you. He said that the Lord your God would give you a place to live. So, he has given you this land east of the Jordan River. But now you must help your relatives get their land. **14)** Your wives and children can stay here with your animals. But all your fighting men must prepare for battle and lead the men of the other tribes across the river. **15)** The Lord has given you a place to live, and he will do the same for your brothers. But you must help them until they take control of the land the Lord your God is giving them. Then you can come back and settle here on the east side of the river. This is the land that the Lord's servant Moses said would be yours."

What is God asking you to do, reference to Joshua's calling? And list the areas of assignments? (Please explain)

_____

_____

What is the battle you are facing? and Why? (Please explain)

_____

_____

Where are you tempted to be afraid? And Why? (Please explain)

_____

_____

Where are you prone to be discouraged? And Why? (Please explain)

_____

_____

Deuteronomy 31:6, AMP, "Be strong and courageous, do not be afraid or tremble in dread before them, for it is the Lord your God who goes with you. He will not fail you or abandon you."

I. **Looking at this caption of the cat, what do you see?**
   _____

   1. What act of courage have you ever witnessed?
      _____
      _____

   2. What are some of the ordinary, day-to-day acts of courage that people perform without ever being noticed?
      _____
      _____

II. **The Word of God**

   2 Timothy 1:7-12 AMP

   7) For God did not give us a spirit of timidity or cowardice or fear, but **[He has given us a spirit]** of power and of love and of sound judgment and personal discipline **[abilities that result in a calm, well-balanced mind and self-control.]** 8) So do not be ashamed to testify about our Lord or about me His prisoner, but with me take your share of suffering for the gospel **[continue to regardless of the circumstances]**, in accordance with the power of God **[for His power is invincible]**, 9) for He delivered us and saved us and called us with a holy calling **[a calling that leads to a consecrated life—a life set apart—a life of purpose]**, not because of our works [or because of any personal merit—we could do nothing to earn this], but because of His own purpose and grace **[His amazing, undeserved favor]** which was granted to us in Christ Jesus before the world began **[eternal ages ago]**, **10)** but now **[that extraordinary purpose and grace]** has been fully disclosed and realized by us through the appearing of our Savior Christ Jesus who **[through His incarnation and earthly ministry]** abolished death **[making it null and void]** and brought life and immortality to light through the gospel, **11)** for which I was appointed a preacher and an apostle and a teacher **[of this good news regarding salvation]. 12)** This is why I suffer as I do. Still, I am not ashamed; for I know Him **[and I am personally acquainted with Him]**

*whom I have believed [**with absolute trust and confidence in Him and in the truth of His deity**], and I am persuaded [**beyond any doubt**] that He is able to guard that which I have entrusted to Him until that day [**when I stand before Him.***

1. **Apostle Paul exhibits a spirit of courage and deep commitment in this passage. What seems to drive or motivate him to remain courageous?**

   _____

   _____

   _____

   _____

   _____

2. **How is the example of Paul challenging or moving you to want to be more courageous?**

   _____

   _____

   _____

   _____

3. **This passage says God does not put a spirit of "timidity" or cowardice in His Followers.**

4. **Illustrate what you think a spirit of timidity looks like in one of these areas:**

   - **Marriage**
   - **Friendship**
   - **Marketplace**
   - **Raising Children**

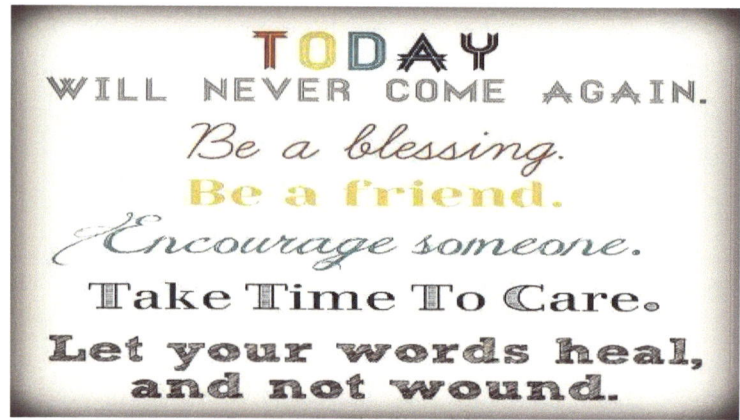

Inside the Box
Spiritual Courage

Let us break down the dimensions of courage so we can understand the purpose of this word. If we can dissect this word "courage" thoroughly, it will not be challenging to apply it to our kingdom lifestyle. Courage is effective in one's life when wisdom and understanding are inserted into the saint's hearts. Then courage will release its roots into the foundation by faith that produces boldness in pursuing your ultimate goal.

With this in mind, Satan cannot deceive or trick you into fear.

Please answer these questions list below to the best of your knowledge. There is no wrong answer, simply desires to know your challenges and how you overcome your fear.

1. Since the beginning of your new birth in God's Kingdom, what are some of the challenges you face after you decided to "deny yourself "and follow Jesus? (Minimal of 5 sentences)

_____
_____
_____
_____
_____
_____
_____

Mark 8:34 AMP, "Jesus called the crowd together with His disciples, and said to them, "if anyone wishes to follow Me [as My disciple], he must deny himself [set aside selfish interests], and take up his cross [expressing a willingness to endure whatever may come] and follow Me [believing in Me, conforming to My example in living and, if need be, suffering or perhaps dying because of faith in Me.]" (Emphasis Here)

2. How **courage** in the kingdom lifestyle demand from you in these areas below:

- Educational Institutions
- Employment
- Outreach and In-Reach Evangelism
- Department of Transportations
- Marriage/Family
- And in the Marketplace

_____

_____

_____

_____

_____

_____

*1 Corinthians 13:11 – 13 ERV – 11) When I was a child, I talked like a child, I thought like a child, and I made plans like a child. When I became a man, I stopped those childish ways. 12) It is the same with us. Now we see God as if we are looking at a reflection in a mirror. But then, in the future, we will see him right before our eyes. Now I know only a part, but at that time I will know fully, as God has known me. 13) So these three things continue **faith, hope, and love**. And the **greatest** of these is **love**.*

MORAL COURAGE

I see COURAGE, Do You?

Moral Courage is looking at you in the Mirror:

According to the custom of his time, David was armed only with his sling and shepherd's staff; yet he early gave proof of his strength and courage in protecting his charge. Afterward describing these encounters, he said: "When there came a lion, or a bear, and took a lamb out of the flock, I went out after him, and smote him, and delivered it out of his mouth: and when he arose against me, I caught him by the beard, and smote him, and slew him."

1 Samuel 17:34 - 47 AMPC **(Emphasis Here)**

***vs. 34**; But David said to Saul, "Your servant was tending his father's sheep. When a lion or a bear came and took a lamb out of the flock, **35)** I went out after it and attacked it and rescued the lamb from its mouth; and when it rose up against me, I seized it by its whiskers and struck and killed it. **36)** Your servant has killed both the lion and the bear; and this uncircumcised Philistine will be like one of them since he has taunted and defied the armies of the living God." **37)** David said, "The Lord who rescued me from the paw of the lion and from the paw of the bear, He will rescue me from the hand of this Philistine." And Saul said to David, "Go, and may the Lord be with you." **38)** Then Saul dressed David in his garments and put a bronze helmet on his head, and put a coat of mail **(armor)** on him. **39)** Then fastened his sword over his armor and tried to walk, **[but he could not,]** because he was not used to them. And David* said to Saul, "I cannot go with these, because I am not used to them." So David took them off. **40)** Then he took his *[shepherd's]* staff in his hand and chose for himself five smooth stones out of the stream bed, and put them in his shepherd's bag which he had, that is, in his shepherd's pouch. With his sling in his hand, he approached the Philistine. **41)** The Philistine came and approached David, with his shield-bearer in from of him. **42)** When the Philistine liked around and saw David, he derided and disparaged him because he was *[just]* a young man, with a ruddy complexion, and a handsome appearance. **43)** The Philistine said to David, "Am I a dog; that you come to me with *[Shepherd's]* staffs?" And the Philistine cursed David by his gods. **44)** The Philistine also said to David, "Come to me, and I will give your flesh to the birds of the sky and the beasts of the field." **45)** Then David said to the Philistine, "You come to me with a sword, a spear, and a javelin, but I come to you in the name of the Lord of hosts, the God of the armies of Israel, whom you have taunted. **46)** This day the Lord will hand you over to me, and I will strike you down and cut off your head. And I will give the corpses of the army of the Philistines this day to the birds of the sky and the wild beasts of the earth, so that all the earth may know that there is a God in Israel, **47)** and that this entire assembly may know that the Lord does not save with the sword or with the spear; for the battle is the Lord's and He will hand you over to us."

3. What does moral courage look like in one of these areas: (Use Extra Sheet)

   - Are you challenged the most when you are alone
   - When sexual temptation is your weakness
   - When caught in a temptation unexpectedly
   - Bending the truth when avoiding a conflict
   - Do the mountains of challenges you face in your daily life overwhelm you.
   - Raising your children
   - Loving your spouse during difficult times
   - Integrity towards God's House of Prayer
   - Budget your household expenses together
   - Family Quality Time Together

4. How and where in your lifestyle are you being pressured to surrender morally and fail to exercise courage. Please explain! (use extra sheet of paper)

Confident courage towards a strong Relationship.

How many times do you hear a question about your marriage? Questions like; how did you meet her or him? What attracted you to him or her? What is some of your strength and weakness to help guide a successful covenant agreement? The answer is always intimacy! A solid and sound commitment of confidence in trust. You are building strong valves through communications. Learning likes and dislikes by respecting one's desires. It takes an enormous amount of confidence to become vulnerable and self-disclosing.

A confidence in courage is mandatory for authentic relationships between relatives, neighbors, community, marketplaces, and kingdom family. (Emphasis Here)

How do you see confidence and courage to build a healthy life in relationships?

_____

Explain a time you have seen doubt and unbelief undermine and damage a relationship.

_____

What is one area of your life you need to strengthen by encouraging more confidence in maintaining a sound relationship?

_____

What is one thing you will do to strengthen your confidence and courage? (Please explain)

_____

Facing Challenges:

Growing in confidence always has something to do with seen and unseen challenges that sometimes cause you to think twice before you react.

Confident people are ordinary like you and me who face their fears when challenges appear. They learned when challenges of fear confront them; they will not retreat but advance their will.

Special Assignment

Take some time out during this week to identify one specific area in which you are dealing with a lack of confidence. How do you handle these challenges head-on, and what measures have you taken to overcome them? (Use Extra Sheet)

_____

_____

Memory Truth:

2 Timothy 4:7 AMPC, "I have fought the good **(worthy, honorable, and noble)** fight, I have finished the race, I have kept **(firmly held)** the faith.

Self-Discipline:

> Explain a challenge you have been confronting and dealing with since your last Kingdom Character Training class session.

_____

_____

> What is the meaning of 2 Timothy 4:7 revealed to you, and how is it applicable to your everyday life? (Please explain)

_____

_____

_____

_____

_____

Pursuing Success:

Suppose you had the opportunity to examine people who have experienced a measure of success in their lives. In each case, I think you would find that discipline played a significant role in almost every instance. On the other hand, if you reviewed the history of people who have experienced a string of setbacks and failures, they would probably offer you a very candid picture of why so many calamities have befallen them. You might hear them say things like, "I didn't keep my eye on the store," I didn't take care of myself," and the list goes on. These so-called phases can be a form of lack of discipline.

People that succeed in life are disciplined, and on the other hand, all people who struggle are undisciplined. Based on my observation, more often, disciplined people lead to positive results. Every goal and dream with a lack of discipline can be undermined and loses its reality.

THE BIG MIRROR: SELF-EVALUATION

The Big Mirror: Self-Evaluation

[Mark where you feel you are located so far in kingdom character training class]

Spiritual discipline *(personal time with God, worship service participation, and kingdom lifestyle/holy/righteousness)*

```
   Very           slightly         disciplined          highly
Undisciplined   disciplined                          disciplined
{_____I_____I_____I_____}
```

Physical discipline *(eating habits, exercise, sleep habits, and taking care of your body)*

```
   Very           slightly         disciplined          highly
Undisciplined   disciplined                          disciplined
{_____I_____I_____I_____}
```

Financial discipline *(budget money, being a cheerful giver in tithing and offerings faithfully and Stewardship)*

```
   Very           slightly         disciplined          highly
Undisciplined   disciplined                          disciplined
{_____I_____I_____I_____}
```

Relational discipline *(spending time communicating, walking in unity, trustworthy, supporting, and covenant agreement)*

| Very Undisciplined | slightly disciplined | disciplined | highly disciplined |

{_____I_____I_____I_____}

In which area are you the strongest?

_____

What do you think helps you stay strong in this area of discipline?

_____

In which area do you need to grow the most?

_____

Describe what you see in this picture below?

_____

_____

[Proverbs 1:1-7 KJV]

1)The proverbs of Solomon the son of David, king of Israel; 2)To know wisdom and instruction; to perceive the words of understanding; 3)To receive the instruction of wisdom, justice, and judgment, and equity, 4)To give subtly to the simple, to the young man knowledge and discretion. 5) A wise man will hear and will increase learning; and a man of understanding shall attain unto wise counsels: 6) to understand a proverb, and the interpretation; the words of the wise, and their dark sayings. 7) The fear of the Lord is the beginning of knowledge, but fools despise wisdom and instruction.

(Emphasis Here)

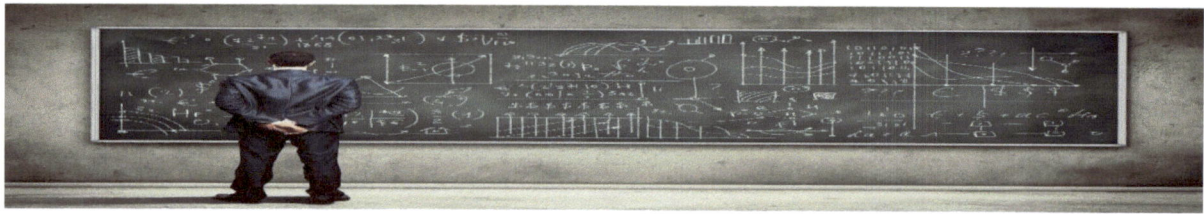

1. What characteristics mark the life of a person who is maturing in wisdom?

2. How do Proverbs connect discipline and wisdom?

3. How would the writer of Proverbs respond to these statements?

    a. A disciplined person is wise!

    b. An undisciplined person is a fool!

4. What area towards your walk with God, do you need intercessors or ministers as confidence builders for you?

5. What are some constructive criticisms they can say or do to help you take steps in those areas of blind spots?

6. Is there anyone you know that would commit themselves completely to challenge you to grow spiritually?

7. How can you constructively be a confidence builder in a person's life?

Balancing on the edge of your character:

What area(s) in your life you lack confidence in?

What will help or encourage you to build confidence?

Challenging yourself to speak before a small or large group.

Challenging yourself to pray when called upon.

Leading a song of praise and worship when asked.

Minister to the lost in outreach evangelism.

Teaching Bible study classes.

Taking a leadership role to lead a group in their kingdom assignment.

Playing an instrument in front of a crowd, small or large.

Preaching or witnessing about the Good News, Gospel of the Kingdom of God the marketplaces.

Confidence Builder in Character adjustment:

Encourage someone in your household who needs to grow in confidence. Can you identify the person(s) in your area of influence?

Listed below and set an objective of guiding them in reaching their growth of confidence.

1. Family: _____

    What will you do to help build confidence in his or her life?

2. A friend _____

    What will you do to help build confidence in his or her life?

Patience: Explain your efforts in a few words being a confidence builder in another person's life.

_____

Looking in the Big Mirror of Patience

Patience with God is an ability to trust and wait on Him in times of challenges and difficulties. Are you seeking The Lord for a breakthrough, and it seems like it will not be on time when you need it?

"He gives strength to the weary and increases the power of the weak. Even the young grow tired and weary, and young men stumble and fall, but those who hope in the Lord will renew their strength. They will soar on wings like eagles; they will run and not grow weary; they will walk and not be faint."

Isaiah 40:29-31 NIV

To be patient is to endure all types of trials and endurance.

Here are five Biblical stories of those who have overcome trials and temptation. It made them stronger as they strive to become patient as they lived out the plan and purpose of God throughout their lives.

1. Joseph - A True example of Patience: Joseph was a man who feared the Lord; God rewarded him for his righteousness. He was sold into slavery by his brothers. (His brothers envied him because of the dream he shared with them). "Judah said to his brothers, "What will we gain if we kill our brother and cover up his blood? Come, let us sell him to the Ishmaelites and not lay our hands on him; after all, he is our brother, our own flesh and blood." His brothers agreed. So, when the Midianite merchants came by, his brothers pulled Joseph up out of the cistern and sold him for twenty shekels of silver to the Ishmaelites, who took him to Egypt." ***Genesis 37:26-28 NIV*** Joseph patiently worked faithfully in every situation of challenges. He waited for God to fulfill the promise of raising him up to be a leader for his people. Through Joseph's patience and perseverance, God raised him up to a position of great power and authority. Joseph ruled over Egypt and his people. So, we see how patience was needed for all the Lord promised to accomplish in Joseph and his family's life.

2. Abraham - The Father of Many Nations: God promised Abraham that he would be the Father of many nations. "The Lord had said to Abram, "Go from your country, your people, and your father's household to the land I will show you. "I will make you into a great nation, and I will bless you; I will make your name great, and you will be a blessing. I will bless those who bless you, and whoever curses you I will curse; and all peoples on earth will be blessed through you." Genesis 12:1-3 NIV Abraham and Sarah have no children; she was barren. In their old age, Abraham (100) and Sarah (90) years conceived a child. It took many years of patience to wait for the promise to be fulfilled and recorded him as a man of faith.

3. Job - A man of Patience: This man was blameless and upright; he feared God and shunned evil." Job was a man who was afflicted with sores all over his body. Job lost his house, sons and daughters, lives stock, despite all the suffering, Job never curses God; he waited for God to shine on him again. As he was going through trusting God for healing and deliverance, his wife encouraged him to curse God and die. But Job continues to endure the most complex trials as a good soldier. He never sins against

God, even though he lost everything. He suffered pain and loss, yet he endured it all. At the end of the story, we learned that God restored to him double-fold for all he lost.

4. Simeon - Awaited Eagerly for the Birth of Jesus: The Holy Ghost revealed to Simeon that he would not see death until he had witnessed the birth of the Messiah. After Jesus arrived in the temple, Simeon was led by the Spirit to visit Him there. Simeon held Jesus in his arms and thanked God for the promise.

5. Jesus Christ - An Example of Patience: Jesus loved and trained the disciples that His Father had given him patiently even though they did not fully understand the Kingdom of God and their purpose in life.

Looking at another angle of the mirror

Explain some of the moments in your life when your patience seemed challenged-the least and the most.

_____

_____

Luke 15:11 – 24 AMP – The Prodigal Son

11) Then He said, *"A certain man had two sons.* **12)** *The younger of them [inappropriately] said to his father, 'Father, give me the share of the property that falls to me.' So he divided the estate between them.* **13)** *A few days later, the younger son gathered together everything [that he had] and traveled to a distant country, and there he wasted His fortune in reckless and immoral living.* **14)** *Now when he had spent everything, a severe famine occurred in that country, and he began to do without and be in need.* **15)** *So he went and forced himself on one of the citizens of that country, who sent him into his fields to feed pigs.* **16)** *He would have gladly eaten the [carob] pods that the pigs were eating [but they could not satisfy his hunger], and no one was giving anything to him.* **17)** *But when he [finally] came to his senses, he said, 'How many of my Father's I have sinned against heaven and in your sight.* **18)** *I will get up and go to my father, and I will say to him, "Father, I have sinned against heaven and in your sight.* **19)** *I am no longer worthy to be called your son; [just] treat me like one of your hired men."* **20)** *So he got up and came to his father. But while he was still a long way off, his father saw him and was moved with* *compassion for him, and ran and embraced him and kissed him. 21) And the son said to him, 'Father, I have sinned against heaven and in your sight; I am no longer worth to be called your son.' 22) But the father said to his servants, 'Quickly bring out the best robe [for the quest of honor] and put it on him; and give him a ring for*

his hand, and sandals for his feet. 23) And bring the fattened calf and slaughter it, and let us [invite everyone and] feast and celebrate; 24) for this son of mine was [as good as] dead and is alive again; he was lost and has been found.' So they began to celebrate.

In this story of the Prodigal Son, as a father, what are some of the possible responses you would have said to your son when he finally returned home?

List **three** responses and explain each one:

- Response number one.

_____

_____

_____

_____

- Response number two.

_____

_____

_____

_____

- Response number three.

_____

_____

_____

_____

1. Describe the father's character in this story in {3} sentences.

_____
_____
_____
_____
_____
_____

2. In this story, how does God relate His incredible patience of confidence toward us? {3} sentences.

_____
_____
_____
_____
_____
_____

Deeper Look in the Mirror

Lack of Patience:

A husband or wife was wounded by being attacked verbally, then later hoping they will forget what was said. But the words from his or her mouth can be so horrifying that it is difficult for them to ignore. ***Proverbs 18:21 AMP – Death and life are in the power of the tongue, and those who love it and indulge it will eat its fruit and bear the consequences of their words.*** Their words penetrated their hearts, and they could not shake it off. Suppose a Dad yells at his son, and Mom hollers at her daughter without taking the time to explain to them in a passionate voice of understanding. In that case, it will cause significant damage to the child's confidence and relationship with their parents. ***Proverbs 22:6 AMP – Train up a child in the way he should go [teaching him to seek God's wisdom and will for his abilities and talents]; even when he is old, he will not depart from it.*** They will view them as having character issues, and they will be afraid to come to them with real problems, and it will lead them outside of the home to talk to someone else about the issues they are experiencing.

Impatience is the root of all your problems. You can't force yourself on people to give you instant answers. It's very imperative to let them unfold before you.

1. Has there ever been a time in your life that your parents or elderly family members verbally abused you? Please explain?

_____

_____

_____

_____

2. How did you feel deep inside at that very moment? Please explain where it hurts the most.

_____

_____

_____

_____

This subject of patience can be very sensitive. If there is any pain, hurt, or un-forgiveness that you have been holding for a long time, you must let it go **NOW** so you can become free, moving forward in the character of God. Your testimony is much needed in the kingdom in helping others to overcome their disappointments.

Let us take this time (10 minutes) praying for each other. Let's pray for complete healings for those who have experienced pain or disappointment with impatient person(s) or relatives.

Then allow a time for confession and forgiveness of the times you have wounded others through being impatient.

Understanding God's patience with unbelievers

As you mature into the knowledge of God's Word, you will learn of the depth of His patience towards people who are dealing with the sin of rebellion and pride. From Genesis to Revelation the Bible contains the history of the human race's rebellion and disobedience. As a Holy God, He could have eliminated all offenders, exterminated the whole human race. However, He still loves us and seeks to enter into a loving relationship with us.

How does your prayer life build your relationship with God?

_____

_____

How can you have a good relationship with God?

_____

_____

Psalms 103:8 AMP, "The Lord is merciful and gracious, Slow to anger and abounding in compassion and lovingkindness."

When His Church **(a living organism)** remembers the Lord's patience with us and with all who are still disobedient, we are called to share in the same loving patience He shows us.

Explain how God was patient with you in one of these areas below:
- Your attitude and behavior among family
- Your words of reflection
- Your attitude and behavior in the Marketplace
- Your relationship with God

_____

_____

_____

_____

_____

_____

_____

God's patience with Believers

Did you know our Heavenly Father was very patient with us before we accepted Him as our Lord and Savior. His patience continues guiding, training, and discipling us through the Holy Spirit. When we read about Peter's relationship with Jesus, we see how Peter communicates with Jesus in the natural realm more than the spirit realm. Therefore, Peter challenged Jesus' patience. Peter was very outspoken more than the other disciples, but sometimes his mouth led him to error. Through it all, Jesus continued to love him.

Matthew and Mark's accounts are an almost identical telling of when Jesus approached their fishing boats. But Luke adds more detail, painting a picture of Peter and Jesus having a sincere moment at the very beginning of their relationship. Upon seeing the miracle of fish on a fishing trip, Peter realizes his sinful state of mind and gives glory to the Lord before him by falling to his knees.

Luke 5:8 AMP, "But when Simon Peter saw this, he fell down at Jesus' knees, saying, 'Go away from me, for I am a sinful man, O Lord!'"

Luke 5:10b AMP, "Jesus said to Simon, 'Have no fear; from now on you will be catching men!'"

After hearing Jesus's words, Peter and the other three stop their occupation as a fisherman and begin following Jesus. Along their journey with Jesus, Peter continued to make mistakes, but Jesus, as is His nature, loved Peter wholeheartedly and continued to use him in His kingdom's work.

*Luke 9:20 AMP, "And He said to them, 'But who do you say that I am?' Peter replied, 'The Christ **(the Messiah, the Anointed)** of God!'"*

Everyday people, like Peter, and like you and me, seeing how Jesus took an uneducated, sinful man and loved him enough to give us assurance He can do this for us as well.

Peter was a man who desired a strong faith but faltered often. He stepped onto the rough sea to meet Jesus walking on water, yet even after safely taking steps, he began to allow doubt and unbelief to set in because of unseen distraction.

Matthew 16:21-23, AMP, **21)** *"From that time on Jesus began to show His disciples **[clearly]** that He must go to Jerusalem, and endure many things at the hands of the elders as the chief priests and scribes **(Sanhedrin Jewish High Court)** and be killed, and be raised **[from death to life]** on the third day.* **22)** *Peter took Him aside **[to speak to Him privately]** and began to reprimand His, saying, "May God forbid it! This will never happen to you."* **23)** *But Jesus turned and said to Peter, "Get behind Me, Satan! You are a stumbling block to me; for you are not setting your mind on things of God, but on things of man."*

Later, Peter even rebuked the Lord after He foretold of His death. (Peter's Denials)

Matthew 26:69-75 AMP, **69)** *"Now Peter was sitting outside in the courtyard and a servant girl came up to him and said, "You too were with Jesus the Galilean."* **70)** *But he denied it before them all saying, "I do not know what you are talking about."* **71)** *And when he had gone out to the gateway, another servant girl saw him and she said to the bystanders, This man was with Jesus the Nazarene."* **72)** *And again he denied it with an oath, "I do not know the man."* **73)** *After a little while the bystanders came up and said to Peter, "Surely you are one of them too; for even your **[Galilean]** accent gives you away."* **74)** *Then he began to curse **[that is, to invoke God's judgment on himself]** and swear **[an oath]**, "I do not know the man!" And at that moment a rooster crowed.* **75)** *And Peter remembered the **[prophetic]** words of Jesus, when He had said, "Before a rooster crows, you will deny Me three times." And he went outside and wept bitterly **[in repentance]**.*

True repentance will allow the Holy Spirit to soften our hearts so The Lord's patience can work within us freely. He will quietly replace us with an attitude of open-mindedness, wisdom, and understanding.

- By reading the previous scriptures, we see how He showed patience with Peter in the middle of all his inconsistency. What is one inconsistent area of your life that God is extending patience to today?

- What needs to happen for you to become more consistent in this above area or areas?

- What is one situation in your life in which you struggle with impatience?

- How can your Leader's of the Five-Fold Ministry support you as you seek the influence of the Kingdom of God in living a life of patience?

Yourself in the Mirror

Honest confession – Exercise Moment:

- If there is a person(s) you have been impatient with, contact that person and reconcile your impatience with them.
- Let them know the Holy Spirit is working on your character traits in your life.
- Let them know you seek the Kingdom of God and Righteousness to live with a deeper level of patience.
- Please keep you in prayer that His Will be done in your life.

Self- Reflection from becoming more patient:

As you look in the mirror, how has the Holy Spirit developed patience in your life up to this point of the Kingdom Training? Please answer in (5) sentences!

- If you asked anyone for forgiveness for your impatience in the past, how did they respond? Please answer in (5) sentence

- What impact has this had on your relationship with others?

Mirror of Reflection

If you were to take a personal inventory of your life's history, what is one thing you shouldn't have quit? Please see the list below and explain.

_____

_____

_____

- Salvation
- Ministry
- Marriage
- Education

- Occupation
- Marketplace
- Leadership
- Driving
- Flying
- Boating
- Camping
- Hunting
- Recreation
- Other Hobby

Putting Yourself in the Mirror

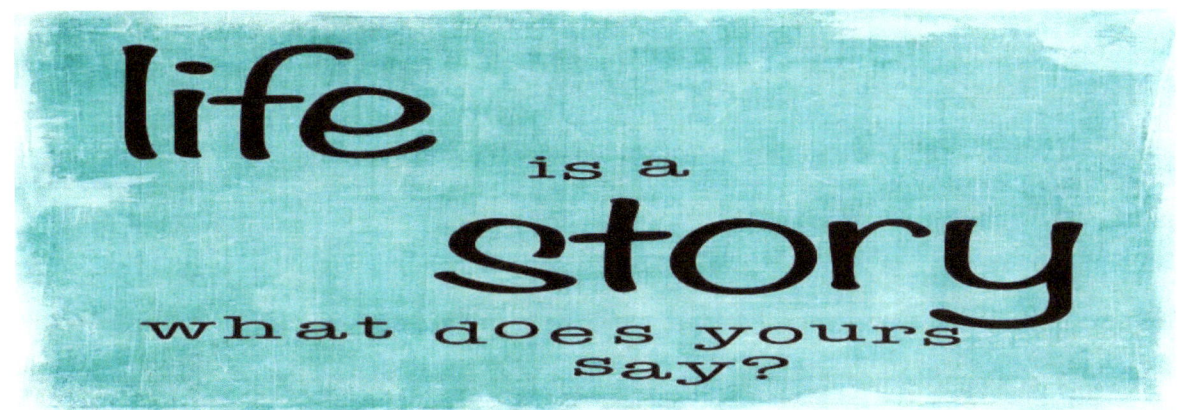

Impartation from a Patient Father

Luke 15:11-24 ERV (Story About Two Sons)

11) Then Jesus said, "There was a man who had two sons. 12) The younger son said to his father, 'Give me now the part of your property that I am supposed I am supposed to receive someday.' So the father divided his wealth between his two sons. 13) "A few days later the younger son gathered up all that he had and left. He traveled far away to another country, and there he wasted his money living like a fool. 14) After he spent everything he had, there was a terrible famine throughout the country. He was hungry and needed money. 15) So he went and got a job with one of the people who lived there. The man sent him into the fields to feed pigs. 16) He was so hungry that he wanted to eat the food the pigs were eating. But no one gave him anything. 17) The son realized that he had been very foolish. He thought, 'All my father's hired workers have plenty of food. But here I am, almost dead because I have nothing to eat. 18) I will leave and go to my father. I will say to him: Father, I have sinned against God and have done wrong to you. 19) I am no longer worthy to be called your son. But let me be like one of your hired workers.' 20) So he left and went to his father.

The Younger Son Returns

*"While the son was still a long way off, his father saw him coming and felt sorry for him so he ran to him and hugged and kissed him.**21)** The son said, 'Father, I have sinned against God and have done wrong to you. I am no longer worthy to be called your son.'**22)** "But the father said to his servants, 'Hurry'! Bring the best clothes and put them on him. Also, put a ring on his finger and good sandals on his feet.**23)** And bring our best calf and kill it so that we can celebrate with plenty to eat.**24)** My son was dead, but now he is alive again! He was lost, but now he is found! So they began to have a party.*

This story is called "The Parable of the Prodigal Son." Here we know God is the Father, and He is patient beyond our understanding. He is always waiting for us to return with an open arm. He is never impatient with us because He loved us so much.

In the coming weeks, take time to identify one or two situations where you find yourself impatient. If the Lord walked into your mindset at that very moment, how do you think He will respond? What character adjustment will he bring? As you pick up your mirror and look at yourself while He is ministering, begin to pray for inner strength to enter a place of renewal spirit of patience that will reflect your heart in kingdom character.

A Forgiving Father, who loves us FOREVER

Confession is good for the inner core of your being, The Soul Realm.

If there is a person or persons you have offended recently or in the past, contact them and make it right. Get rid of the spirit of pride and humble yourself toward patients in regaining and respecting them. Let them know that The Lord is working on your behalf in character development whereby character traits are reinvested within you. Seeking first the Kingdom of God and righteousness will develop you into a deeper level of patience as you dress up in the armor of God.

Endurance.

How has the Holy Spirit, who is our Teacher, helped you develop the characteristic of patience in your life since you have been attending this training? (10 – Sentences, please)

_____

_____

_____

_____

_____

_____

_____

_____

_____

_____

If you notified someone and ask forgiveness for being impatient with them, how did they respond? What impact has this had on your relationship? (10 – Sentences, please)

Looking at **Endurance** in the Mirror:

The Word of God teaches us not to live in the past. But sometimes, it pays to consider the high price of quitting. Many people in your family, local assembly, neighborhoods, and business have scars from having quit on someone or something. They will look back on their lives and these thoughts could come:

- Why did I stop so easily?
- It's easier not to go to Character Training sessions than to keep going week after week.
- It's easier to keep on sleeping for another 15 minutes than to get up early for work.
- It's easier to avoid a heated confrontation from a spouse than to stay and work out the misunderstanding.
- It's easier to get up on Sunday morning to watch CNN, MSNBC, and FOX NEWS,

LOCAL NEWS and sip on some hot tea or coffee than waking up the rest of the family, making sure everyone is dressed and driving to the House of Prayer.
- Simply, it's just too easy just to quit.

As you look back over your life, what is one thing you wish you would not have given up on? Please explain.

_____

_____

James 1:1-4, 12 ERV

> *1) Greetings from James, a servant of God and of the Lord Jesus Christ. To God's people who are scattered all over the world. 2) My brothers and sisters, you will have many kinds of trouble. But this gives you a reason to be very happy. 3) You know that when your faith is tested, you learn to be patient in suffering. 4) If you let that patience work in you, the end result will be good. You will be mature and complete. You will be all that God wants you to be. 12) Great blessings belong to those who are tempted and remain faithful! After they have proved their faith, God will give them the reward of eternal life. God promised this to all people who love him.*

2) In these verses above, James walks us through a process of growing in maturity. What are the elements of this process? Please explain.

3) Why is endurance an essential part of this process? Please explain.

4) James invites us to *"consider it pure joy"* when we face struggles that demand endurance. This seems like an unlikely attitude for people facing trials and challenging times. How is it possible to experience deep joy while persevering through a challenging experience? (Please explain)

> *5) When I look back on my life, I see pain, mistakes and heartache.*
> *6) When I look in the mirror, I see strength, learned lessons, and pride in myself.*

Don't change yourselves to be like the people of this world, but let God change you inside with a new way of thinking. Then you will be able to understand and accept what God wants for you. You will be able to know what is good and pleasing to him and what is perfect. Romans. 12:2, ERV

Stop and Think!

Locating your quitting points in the mirror.

When you think of track and field competition, you can either make a strong plan of action in preparing to endure in winning or a little of preparation which will cause you to be defeated before you compete. The more complex the work, the greater the success. No PAIN, No GAIN! It is that simple! You cannot afford your mind to dictate how you feel at that present moment.

2 Timothy 2:5, ERV, "Athletes in a race must obey all the rules to win."

When pressure on the job is mounting because of a very tight deadline to finish draws near, you become more intense because of stress that you are experiencing at the point of quitting, throwing in the towel. Your mind begins to speak to you to stop and find another job somewhere else. You begin to review your old resume, begin to search the internet, or visit a temp agency looking for something more rewarding. Just to get away from a nagging boss, hard to please, always knit-picking over dumb stuff that is not relevant to the job.

Just to start all over again somewhere else when the Holy Spirit did not lead you to do so.

You are a local assembly leader, dissatisfied because of not being allowed to lead a ministry. Pastors show favoritism is what you are feeling. You attend every ministry class, bible study, prayer meeting, outreach ministry, visiting the sick, feeding program, bus ministry, etc. But you have not been allowed to lead a particular ministry at the local assembly. Maybe you might be impatient, and your tolerance level is low. When was the last time you have looked in the mirror? If it was recently, what is it you cannot see? So, if you cannot see it, then the next thing you see is **'QUITTING!'** Giving it all up after you had been in fellowship 2, 4, 6, 8, or 10 years. Instead of looking at yourself in the mirror and asking the Holy Spirit to heal you, you look for an easier and comfortable way out.

When you are engaged in a heated conversation, going back and forth and cannot see an end in sight. You feel the frustration setting within you, and you let all those words push your buttons. Do you allow your emotions to get the best of you? Do you feel like the only way out of this is to simply "QUIT!"

(Sounds like a failing marriage)

Now you are ready to move out, leave or storm out of the picture **however quitting is not the answer!**

Select one of these quitting points you face that is below: Please explain why?

- Physically – Relationally – Morally – Educationally – Spiritually – Professionally

What is a critical point of giving up that challenges you now?

Are you having a difficult time with what you are dealing with at this present moment?

What is stressing you to the point of quitting this training class now?

Breaking through the points of giving up or simply quitting: Is it your feelings or emotions?

Endurance is a critical attribute in our lives that will enable us to develop the character of Jesus Christ. It is imperative to press on or break through these points where so we can endure. *"Thou therefore endure hardness, as a good soldier of Jesus Christ."* 2 Timothy 2:3 KJV. When faithful mile runners feel they can't run another step, they begin to remind themselves that they are not defeated. They get another wind within them and press on. They are disciplined to know, NO PAIN, NO GAIN. *Philippians 4:13, 14, ERV* **13)** *"Christ is the one who gives me the strength I need to do whatever I must do.* **14)** *But it was good that you helped me when I needed help."*

*Matthew 6:33 AMPC, "But seek **(aim at and strive after)** first of all His kingdom and His righteousness **(His way of doing and being right)**, and then all these things taken together will be given you besides." 1 Chronicles 16:11 AMPC, "Seek the Lord and His strength; yearn for and seek His face and to be in His presence continually!"* Knowledge of God's Word is a greater nutrient for our body, soul, and spirit. But wisdom and understanding is a must in balancing your gifts and character in Jesus Christ.

We need to draw on His strength daily striving for perfection and transparency as an overcomer.

WE ARE WINNERS!

*John 16:33 NIV, "I have told you these things, so that in me you may have peace. In this **world** you will have trouble. But take heart! I have **overcome the world**."*

*1 John 5:4 NIV, "for everyone born of God overcomes **the world**. This is **the** victory that has **overcome the world**, even our faith'*

1. When was there a time you endured and crashed through a giving-up moment in your life?

   _____

   _____

2. What did it take to persevere to the point of breaking through this giving-up point? Please explain.

   _____

   _____

3. How did it feel to surrender through this giving-up point?

   _____

   _____

4. What is your thought on this statement: *"Have you almost ever given up or surrendered when you felt like you hit a wall? After you got on the other side of it you discovered that you were giving people a false idea of your true feelings, which is called a character flaw".*

_____

_____

PROCESSING ENDURANCE

The most important first step you will have to consider is to make a strong commitment to yourself and be honest about your constructive development of endurance. This involves establishing a pattern of always pushing yourself beyond where you feel too comfortable. Endurance transpires when things or circumstances occur when they are inconvenient. An inconvenient state of mind will allow you to become more disciplined in endurance. Be aware of a life of convenience, you will end up taking life for granted. Endurance requires **DISCIPLINE** in one's thinking. Develop a new way of thinking and perseverance. It's a kingdom lifestyle we must show the world that we can live a Holy and righteous life. We should all practice discipline until it becomes embedded within our inconvenient way of life. Yes, I said inconvenient because this is the best way of becoming stronger and focused. Your endurance towards your inconvenient state of mind will encourage you on how to live out your true character in Christ Jesus. Nothing will be able to stop your progress in Him. When He calls you, you will say, 'Yes Lord" and "Yes to Your Will and Your Way." Period! Submission for the sake of accountability by His Grace.

*I Peter 5:6-11 AMP, "Therefore humble yourselves under the mighty hand of God **[set aside self-righteous pride]**, so that He may exalt you **[to a place of honor in His service]** at the appropriate time, 7) casting all your cares **[all your anxieties, all your worries, and all your concerns, once and for all]** on Him, for He cares about you **[with deepest affection, and watches over you very carefully]**. 8) Be sober **[well balanced and self-disciplined]**, be alert* and *cautious at all times. That enemy of yours, the devil, prowls around like a roaring lion **[fiercely hungry]**, seeking someone to devour. 9) But resist him, be firm in your faith **[against his attack – rooted, established, immovable]**, knowing that the same experiences of suffering are being experienced by your brothers and sisters throughout the world. **[You do not suffer alone.]** 10) After you have suffered for a little while, the God of all grace **[who imparts His blessing and favor]**, who called you to His own eternal glory in Christ, will Himself complete, confirm, strengthen, and establish you **[making you what you ought to be]**. 11) To Him be dominion **(power, authority, sovereignty)** forever and ever. Amen."*

What are some specific areas in your life you would love to see develop? Please explain each area.

1) _____

_____

2) _____

_____

3) _____

_____

Exercising Endurance Through Discipline

In this moment what specifically have you not put on the table that you are still dealing or wrestling with regards to discipline? Please explain.

_____

_____

_____

_____

What are the stumping blocks in your way? Please explain.

_____

_____

_____

_____

What feelings at a particular time lead you to the point of giving in to your emotions? Please explain.

_____

_____

_____

_____

What area(s) of discoveries have you acknowledged of giving up or throwing in the towel? Please explain.

_____

_____

_____

_____

How can discipline challenge you in breaking through for your healings and deliverance? Please explain.

Let us take a few minutes and praise our Heavenly Father:

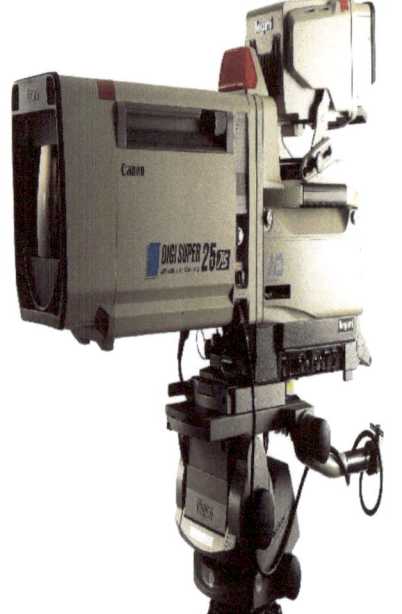

Psalms 28:7 AMP, "The Lord is my strength and my [impenetrable] shield; My heart trusts [with unwavering confidence] in Him, and I am helped; Therefore my heart greatly rejoices, And with my song I shall thank Him and praise Him."

Proverbs 12:19 NIV, "Truthful lips endure forever, but a lying tongue lasts only a moment."

I Corinthians 4:12 NIV, "We work hard with our hands. When we are cursed, we bless; when we are persecuted, we endure it;"

1 Corinthians 10:13 NIV, "No temptation has overtaken you except what is common to mankind. And God is faithful; he will not let you be tempted beyond what you can bear. But when you are tempted, he will also provide a way out so that you can endure it.

2 Timothy 2:12 NIV, "if we endure, we will also reign with him. If we disown him, he will also disown us;"

Hebrews 12:7 NIV, "Endure hardship as discipline; God is treating you as his children. For what children are not disciplined by their father?"

1 Peter 2:20 NIV, "But how is it to your credit if you receive a beating for doing wrong and endure it? But if you suffer for doing good and you endure it this is commendable before God."

Revelation 3:10 NIV, "Since you have kept my command to endure patiently, I will also keep you from the hour of trial that is going to come on the whole world to test the inhabitants of the earth."

*Psalm 103:1-13 ERV, **1)** "My soul, praise the Lord! Every part of me, praise his holy name! **2)** My soul praise the Lord and never forget how kind he is! **3)** He forgives all our sins and heals all our sicknesses. **4)** He saves us from the grave, and he gives us love and compassion. **5)** He gives us plenty of good things. He makes us young again, like an eagle that grows new feathers. **6)** The Lord does what is fair. He brings justice to all who have been hurt by others. **7)** He taught his laws to Moses. He let Israel see the powerful things he can do. **8)** The Lord is kind and merciful. He is **patient** and full of love. **9)** He does not always criticize. He does not stay angry with us forever. **10)** We sinned against him, but he didn't give us the punishment we deserved. **11)** His love for his followers is as high above us as heaven is above the earth. **12)** And he has taken our sins as far away from us as the east is from the west. **13)** The Lord is as kind to his followers as a father is to his children.*

Psalms 103:1-13 ERV

1. According to Psalms 103, what does God provide for you?

   _____
   _____
   _____
   _____

2. How have you experienced the truth in your life relating to Psalms 103?

   _____
   _____
   _____
   _____

3. Describe the heart and character of God?

　

4. How does a discontent **(a person who is dissatisfied, typically with the prevailing social or political situation)** person who is always seeking more from God, look in the mirror of things? Please explain.

SHARPENING YOUR FOCUS IN THE MIRROR

The Myth of more. **Myth** – a popular belief or tradition that has grown up around something or someone. Many of us still believe in the myth of more, so from the list below please explain your point of view.

- More money

_____

_____

- More status

_____

_____

- More authority or power

_____

_____

- More travels

_____

_____

- More excitement or entertainment

_____

_____

Emptiness of the Inner Man (Soul)

Our hearts sometimes become tired or restless until we can find rest in Christ Jesus. It's very true that we have a vacuum or void within our soul until we establish an intimate relationship with our Heavenly Father that only He can fill in our hearts.

What does God mean when He asks you to give Him your heart? Please explain.

_____

_____

_____

_____

_____

_____

Our spiritual and natural hearts are parallel: What happens in the spiritual realm also happens in the natural realm and vice versa. Below are some examples of the heart being in both forms.

Heart of a natural man	Heart of a spiritual man
Located almost on the left side of your chest	Center of your thoughts, words, actions, ministry and motivating everything you do and speak
Nutrients contained in the food consumed by the person	What a person consumes through their mind and experiences. The purest of life is obtained from eating the infallible Word of God.
The heart pumps blood from one end of the body to the other if it is functioning properly.	The heart of a person circulates the life throughout the Body of Christ if he or she is functioning properly.
The heart pumps blood throughout the body, cleansing the body from its impurities.	The heart of a person knows and teaches or preaches the cleansing power of the blood of Jesus Christ, continually purifying the spiritual Body of Christ.
The heart beats automatically, without the conscious effort of a person.	The heart of a person shows the love, joy and peace of God naturally and without any conscious effort or insincerity.
The heart is more prone to disease and attacks when you're on a high fat diet, that leads to obesity.	The heart of a person is more prone to spiritual sickness as he or she takes the rich truths of the Word of God without practicing them and making it an active part of their life.
The heart will be more prone to disease and attack with the more tension and stress a person experiences.	The heart of a person is more prone to spiritual sickness as he or she lives a high-adrenaline, high – stress lifestyle by not entrusting all cares into the Lord's hands.

This parallel of hearts demonstrates the very importance of the spiritual heart in the life of God and The Church *(His Ecclesia)*.

1. Describe what your life was like before you knew the love and forgiveness of Jesus?

   _____

   _____

   _____

2. What were some of the things that you tried to fill the void in your heart with?

   _____

   _____

   _____

3. Is there someone in your life who still has an empty soul and needs to know the love of God?

   _____

   _____

   _____

4. Who is that person?

   _____

   _____

   _____

5. How can you reach out to this person with the love of God?

   _____

   _____

   _____

Fulfillment of the Inner Man (Soul).

Embracing the fulfillment of the inner man is when a person realizes their iniquity and sin have separated them from the love of God. When a person realizes only Jesus Christ can forgive their iniquity and sin and reconcile them back to the Father, they will have to make an eternal decision.

First, let me help you with the difference between iniquity and sin. Most people are greatly concerned about their sin rather than about their iniquity. Both of these must be removed you're your life in order to enter into the Kingdom of Heaven.

Iniquity – in the Webster Merriam Dictionary is defined as "a gross injustice, wickedness, a wicked act or thing or sin." The Hebrew origin of iniquity is: "evil, make crooked, pervert or perverse, bent, in vain, trouble and false." The Greek origin of iniquity is defined as: injustice, unrighteousness, wrong and moral wrongfulness." It also means; quilt, twist, distort, violent deeds of injustice, mischievous purpose, evil plan or consideration."

*Deuteronomy 32:4 KJV, "He is the Rock, his work is perfect: for all his ways are judgment: A God of truth and without **iniquity**, just and right is he.*

*Exodus 32:6-9, AMP, "Then the Lord passed by in front of him, and proclaimed, "The Lord, the Lord God, compassionate and gracious, slow to anger, and abounding in lovingkindness and truth **(faithfulness)**; 7) keeping mercy and lovingkindness for thousands, forgiving iniquity and transgression and sin; but He will by no means leave the guilty unpunished, visiting **(avenging)** the iniquity **(sin, quilt)** of the fathers upon the children and the grandchildren to the third and fourth generations [that is, calling the children to account for the sins of their fathers]." 8) Moses bowed to the earth immediately and worshiped [the Lord]. 9) And he said, If now I have found favor and lovingkindness in Your sight, O Lord, let the Lord, please, go in our midst, though it is a stiff-necked **(stubborn, rebellious)** people, and pardon our iniquity and our sin, and take us as Your possession."*

Psalms 38:18 AMP, "For I do confess my quilt and iniquity; I am filled with anxiety because of my sin.

(When David sinned with Bathsheba)

Psalms 51:2 AMP, "Wash me thoroughly from my wickedness and quilt and cleanse me from my sin.

Sin- an immoral act of transgression against God's divine Law and Order. It is an evil human act of disobedience that violates the nature of man or mankind as well as God's nature and His eternal law. The Hebrew word 'aveira' means 'transgression'. And the word 'avone, or 'iniquity', means a sin done out of moral falling. This word also means to go astray. Sin involves straying from that path.

How has your spouse changed since the void in your heart has been filled with the presence of God?

_____

_____

_____

For the coming days, let us begin to thank our Lord and Savor for entering your heart and life during these Character Training sessions. Continue giving Him all the Glory and Honor for meeting the desires of your hearts and forgiving you from iniquity and sin. Giving Him the praise of showing you how to value your time through discipline, endurance, patience, and relationship with one another.

We would like to take this time to thank you all for your classroom participation in Kingdom Character Training. We pray that these sessions have encouraged, strengthened, motivated, and activated you.

Closing instruction:

Please write a short essay of how this Kingdom Character Training inspires, pushes, searches and digs down deep in the core of your inner man. How did the class motivate you to pursue your destiny in Christ Jesus to become more transparent and discipline you in your character. You have one week to complete, and please turn in your essay to your Leader or Instructor.

Let us pray!

Heavenly Father in Jesus' name, We thank You for spiritual insight and foresight into Your Word of knowing our true identity through the Kingdom Character Training. Knowing and understanding the purpose through Your Word as to why we *"walk by faith and not by sight."* It's our faith that pleases You. As we take this training by grace from the Holy Spirit. May the seed of this Kingdom Character Development Training continue producing the roots of holiness and righteousness in our hearts that will continue to carry us from religion to a relationship with You as we become sons of God in the Earth. We thank you for the grace to endure this discipline training, enable us to do Your Will. In Christ Jesus, we pray, Amen!

About The Blounts

Apostles Terance & Victoria Blount

The Blount's are Founders of Kingdom Reality Ministries, Int'l in Dover, Delaware. They received the mandate as a catalyst in these end-times to build ministry teams through Preaching & Teaching the Gospel of the Kingdom, training and mentoring five-fold leaders, in the marketplace through impartation, workshops, conferences, and Itinerant Preaching/Teaching. Apostle Victoria is the founder of The Kingdom TrailBlazer's Network She also serves as State Representative and Presbytery of Deborah's Global Network for Delaware, Northern Pennsylvania, Maryland, and New Jersey. They both are Global Executive members and USA Trustees of the International Ministers Fellowship (IMF) a Global Network of Ministers & Ministries worldwide.

We profoundly believe God has called us to be a voice to the Body of Christ-Declaring and speaking His mind with The Delivering Power of the Holy Spirit!

In the last days, God says, I will pour out My Spirit on all people. Your sons and daughters will prophesy. Your young men will see visions; your old men will dream dreams. Even on my servants, both men and women, I will pour out my Spirit in those days and they will prophecy: Acts 2:17-18

BIBLICAL REFERENCES

Amplified Bible (AMP)

The Holy Bible, New International Version (NIV)

Holy Bible: Easy-to-Read Version (ERV)

Amplified Bible, Classic Edition (AMPC)

The Jubilee Bible 2000 (JUB)

www.ingramcontent.com/pod-product-compliance
Lightning Source LLC
Chambersburg PA
CBHW061358090426
42743CB00002B/55